Delineation with Astrodynes

Ken Stone

ISBN-10: 0-86690-002-0
IBN-13: 978-0-86690-002-7

First Printing: 1972
Fifth Printing: 2009

Cover Design: Jack Cipolla

Published by:
American Federation of Astrologers, Inc.
6535 S. Rural Road
Tempe, AZ 85285-2040

www.astrologers.com

Printed in the United States of America

Acknowledgement

The author wishes to thank the Church of Light
for permission to use the method
and the information,
as well as many terms and phrases,
regarding astrodynes and delineation,
which are their sole property.

Contents

Introduction

The advent of astrodynes has allowed a greater precision in the natal interpretation of birthcharts. In the old days of astrology the ruler of a chart was taken to be the ruler of the Ascendant. But with a method of mathematically determining the relative power in a horoscope, much of the guesswork is taken out of the interpretation of a chart. Those planets, signs and houses that are strongest can now easily be determined, leading to more accurate determination of vocation, temperament, and compatibility. The harmony or discord will indicate the fortune that can be attracted by each factor. The strongest aspects, and those that have the most harmony and discord, will be found easily.

The onrush of scientific accuracy and technology has made us realize there is a difference between power, which is a potential for action, and harmony, which is the effect of the action. The amount of strength in the chart will show how insistent the desires, or areas of life, are. Whether they express in harmony or with difficulty has little to do with the amount of power it has to accomplish work. In the past—and even too much today—it has been the practice to include such things as essential dignities and one planets "dispositing" another as part of the power a planet has.

Therefore, the first step in a better understanding of how to use astrodynes in a birthchart is to understand what power is in a chart, what harmony is, and the difference between the two.

There are two factors which establish the power of a planet—the house through which the planet is expressing, and the power contributed to it by the aspects. In either case the planetary center of energy is stimulated into action.

The whole principle of essential dignities (home, detriment, etc.) is that each planet finds that a sign's characteristics agree with its characteristics, disagree with the planet's characteristics, or react neutrally. This agreement or disagreement does not add any power. It does not stimulate additional action. Essential dignities merely add to or detract from the fortune of the expression when stimulated.

Since we are talking about planetary energies—and these are what map the individual's own mental makeup—we can make two brief statements about power and harmony. *Power* is the amount of desire energy which is pushing an individual to act. *Harmony* is the quality of the reaction to the actions shown by the power. (Harmony is used to indicate both harmony and discord; in fact, discord is a lack of harmony.)

We can say, then, that any factor in the chart that does not add to the person's drive to action does not add to the power. Any factor which adds to a harmonious or discordant reaction does not add to the power, just increases or decreases the harmony of the reaction.

The important thing that must be realized by the user of astrodynes who would use them proficiently is that astrodyne power is an indicator of the strength of the desires in the individual. If there is one thing that working with astrodynes should contribute to the consciousness of the astrologer, it is to show the patterns of energy working within the individual and the fact that each individual is a composite of various energy centers in a relative state of strength.

When it comes to ability, power is important. Few people have made a success with a weak planet's ability. No matter how much harmony a planet has, if its strength is little, other desires and events will crowd out the ability. If there is not enough strength in the chart, it is bad astrology to advise a person to follow a particular line of work or action simply because there is harmony. The harmony will show good fortune in regard to the planet, but in order to get this fortune the planet must be able to express. If it does not have much power, it will get less chance.

We examine the planets, signs, houses, and the aspects separately. Then, we examine some factors of delineation as astrodynes help do a detailed job. Lastly we examine some thoughts about progressions.

We must close this introduction with this important admonition again:

Each person has the planetary centers of energy in them operating at relative strength to each other. The birthchart pictures this personal makeup. Astrodynes tell us the amount. *In all cases*, our analyses are of personal *energies* that are prompting the individual to act in a certain manner. If we are to understand a person, we must realize this map shows the feelings and thoughts of the individual—and these are live and active factors, not words of description.

Chapter 1

Planets

*W*e cannot really say that any one factor (sign, aspect, planet, house) in a chart is "most important," for all four factors constitute a whole and any one of them missing makes for an impossible situation in life as it is on earth. Nevertheless, a source of power is necessary to start a car. In a similar manner the planetary energies indicate the active desires in the individual. Without these urges the other three factors would cease to have a reason for existence. Without a drive for significance a soul has no reason for life. Twelve signs indicate twelve ways the urge can express; twelve houses indicate twelve departments of life that it can express in; ten aspects indicate ten ways in which other urges can affect the significance (of whatever urge is being analyzed). In each case the key is the drive for significance and its reaction.

This analysis holds true with each planet. Therefore, the relative strength of the planet indicates the relative predominance of the particular urges. For review, then, we consider the effects of each planet when it is dominant, irrespective of the other areas and factors in the chart.

Sun

When the Sun is dominant, the drive for significance is the strongest desire in the chart. The greatest portion of the energy spent will be in the expression which brings esteem, or in the attainment of that esteem. Some will crave the esteem of others. Some will be satisfied with self-esteem. Most people will prefer a bit of both, depending on the harmony which is more satisfying. Temperament, abilities will be those which create a position of importance for the individual. It will be important to dominate the environment and the situation it presents. Harmonious actions will get, quite naturally, a spontaneous following; discordant actions will produce the effect of domination.

Regardless of where it is located in the birthchart the dominant Sun will produce as the guiding light in the life the need to attain esteem and the tendency to measure all actions by the yardstick of how much it contributes to the esteem of the individual. The individuality is all important. The particular house occupied indicates the primary area of experience, the area where the temperament and individuality are most directly located and reached.

A point to be made here, good for all planets, is that a dominant planet will affect temperament regardless of house. The house occupied indicates the department of life that the house represents is most often and strongly concerned with the temperament. In other words, where a dominant planet is located indicates the area of life whose influence in response to the planet is a major factor in the life. Consequently a dominant planet in, say, the eighth house, indicates that the area of life where the primary focus of the dominant urges is, is partner's money, debts, insurance, death, regeneration of desires, and psychic influences. These will play an important part in many of the individual's activities because the dominant planet, when stimulated, has its primary outlet in this house.

Moon

A dominant Moon at birth will not, believe it or not, give a dominant mentality. It will give a person to whom the myriad fluctuating impressions from within or without are of prime importance. It will give a person to whom the understanding and sympathy with people are important. And it will produce a person whose domestic wants and desires are strong. Moods will be a large part of the reaction with a dominant Moon. Constant changing of the mind is a strong possibility, though a variety of other overriding factors can tone it down some. A keynote to the life will be fluctuation. Abilities predominating here are those of sympathetic rapport, understanding, and a desire to take care of those less fortunate. Greatest good will be obtained in this manner.

Mercury

A dominant Mercury indicates one who has his mind constantly in gear at high speeds. It indicates a person who lives largely within the objective mind: thinking, studying, tabulating. He who has Mercury dominant must express himself often. Talking or writing, these individuals are constantly expressing themselves. This individual is one who cannot let his mind succumb to outside influences and, to the extent possible, the emotions from within. To have relevance, events and conditions must yield to reason. Everybody thinks, but to a person with a dominant Mercury the thinking process and the expression of its results are all important.

Venus

A dominant Venus will indicate a person to whom the expression and reception of affection is important. Beauty is an important feature in the life. Venus itself does not necessarily confer artistic talent or a talent for making things of beauty. It does confer a sense of the beautiful - a feeling or appreciation of it. Cheerfulness and conviviality will be stronger than other considerations. Because of this, people will feel like giving attention and favors. There is a tendency to sit back and do as little as possible, since the dominant Venus gets used to the favors done for it. Music, art, and gaiety and entertainment do much for the emotional mood of the Venus individual.

Mars

A dominant Mars indicates a great deal of brute energy awaiting direction. This prodigious energy may go into activities which involve construction and/or the use of the hands and muscles; it may involve hasty action and accidental difficulty; it may be damned up from physical activity and express as anger and irritation; it may express as initiative and ambition. The person with this planet dominant will feel impelled to express with quickness and energy. The animal tendencies and the combative urge will be very strong. There will always be a searching for the next obstacle to hurdle, the next battle to be won.

4

Jupiter

A dominant Jupiter gives the person a jovial attitude and a faith that things will work well. In those religiously inclined, the faith will be in a higher power. In those more materialistically inclined, it will be faith in one's abilities and a confidence that things will go well. The true confidence inspired by a faith in powers greater than the individual is an infectious mood which attracts the attention of those who can do much for the individual; it attracts the patronage of those who hold power. This person has the ability to sell others on himself or whatever he wishes to sell, be it goods, ideas, or good will.

Saturn

A dominant Saturn gives an introspective, serious, economical person. Primary among the objectives of this individual are the safety of himself and those who are under his responsibility. Economy and organization are watchwords, and the natural caution may carry this to an excessive extent, producing foolish hoarding and selfishness. Systematic approaches to a problem are the only ways Saturn knows. A bargain is a bargain and nothing else will do, is Saturn's contention. Lack of material possessions and self-centeredness come from the excessive urge for safety with a dominant Saturn. Consequently, the Saturn has difficulty in taking advantage of opportunities. On the other side of the coin, it truly knows how to save.

Uranus

A dominant Uranus indicates an individual who is inclined to erratic actions. There is a strong tendency to change at a moment's notice, without a great deal of seeming reason. The strong electromagnetic energy generated by Uranus gives a personal magnetism that can attract many people and, consequently, whatever fortune—good or bad—befalls Uranus, it happens through contact with others. Sudden changes of opinion are evident, and events happen suddenly because the reactions change. Whatever happens, the individual's mental horizons are wider. Though there is not always interest in the same, a dominant Uranus can provide a strong sensitivity to occult forces and a sharp intuition. Uranus prompts the attitude of changing the mold of things that are, and to this end it can become too dedicated, to the point of destroying whatever cooperation is necessary to accomplish the task.

Neptune

A dominant Neptune gives an individual with a very strong imagination. It gives a person with extreme sensitivity to the inner planes, and to scenes and energies found there. This person is strongly inclined to be very dramatic in everything they do. There is a tendency for the person to withdraw from the outer world of "reality" to an inner world of their own, where everything is the way they want it to be. The extreme sensitivity causes a tendency to presume things that aren't really so—and the imagination elaborates. This sensitivity of the nervous system makes for easy upsets. This person always expects a little more out of life than life is actually capable of giving.

Pluto

A dominant Pluto indicates a person of dramatic temperament. It is a person whose aims in life depend upon the help and cooperation of others. He will many times urge this cooperation so hard he compels others to do what he wants. He can be very concerned with the welfare of the greatest number of people. If he ever loses this mood of attitude, he can go the opposite way and do almost anything that will undermine the best efforts of humanity. Whichever way is chosen, there is always a strong driving desire—a compulsion to accomplish what is desired. A person with Pluto dominant has a very tensely tuned nervous system—high sensitivity. They are especially sensitive to the thoughts of others, both on the physical plane and the inner planes.

Summary

Having covered briefly what each planet is like if it is dominant, we can then say in a chart that such an attitude will predominate in the individual regardless of sign and department of life. The sign will indicate the method by which it expresses, and the house shows the area of life the dominant desire will most often be expressed. The nature of each planet as given will be noted to predominate the life of the individual regardless of the area of life that gives it maximum opportunity to express.

It is important to consider the dominance of planets just from this point of view, even before applying its effect to the other steps of judging a horoscope because the dominant energies show the predominating desires, which are the key to the individual life pattern.

There is another point to be considered before we leave the planets. Some charts have one planet exceptionally strong. Some may have two. Still others may have three to five planets nearly the same power. The chart that has one planet stronger by far than the others indicates the individual who has one set of abilities strong, and these desires have little competition for development. Those with several planets nearly the same strength as the dominant planet have capacities and desire equally strong and will find it necessary to express all of them. This person seldom develops abilities to their highest, since there are several constantly and nearly equally urging for expression.

There is need for both types of individual. The point is: Do not expect the person with many strong planets to develop the single-mindedness of purpose of the person with one planet exceptionally strong. Conversely, don't expect the person with one planet exceptionally strong to be as versatile as the person with several planets nearly equal.

Chapter 2

Signs and Houses

Signs

*T*he signs are the sounding boards—they create the timbre. Is that sound a flute, a piano, a violin, or trumpet? The same note on all four sounds different while still being the same note. The signs map the method of expression, the particular bias or mode of expression of the original planetary energy. Analysis of signs gives us the predominating methods of expression shown in the life.

Let us quickly recapitulate what effect each sign, when dominant, will have.

Aries

A dominant Aries indicates a predominance of need to express rulership, self-interest, and to start new things. It indicates a tendency to express with zeal and impatience.

Taurus

A dominant Taurus indicates an individual whose guiding light is possessiveness. The individual enjoys the pleasures and leisures of life. He will be hard-working and stubborn; slow but sure.

Gemini

A dominant Gemini indicates the individual who is always engaged in mental pursuit, whether it be gathering information from book, movie, or person; or expressing the knowledge already found in great detail.

Cancer

A dominant Cancer indicates an individual who is extremely sensitive to his environment and therefore resistant to its change. He is moody, impressionable and psychic in a somewhat mediumistic manner.

Leo

A dominant Leo notes the individual who has to be the leader, to be at the center of things. This person is fond of expressing himself in a grandiose manner, making for an entertaining person, if not a leader.

Virgo

A dominant Virgo shows the individual who must break things down into their individual components. He will constantly analyze and criticize, and will be found to have a great store of individual pieces of knowledge.

Libra

A dominant Libra shows one who must have harmony at all costs. A fastidious person who dislikes injustice because it implies unequal opportunity and lack of proper balance, this person will place high value on beauty.

Scorpio

A dominant Scorpio gives an individual who is highly resourceful and doubly persistent. He will have great powers of recuperation. He will have extremely active likes and dislikes and will not easily forget or easily forgive what is done against him. He will tackle dirty jobs.

Sagittarius

Sagittarius dominant shows a person of outspoken words. He will perceive the relationships of many things and express with a candor that sometimes will shock others. He loves the outdoors and sporting or playtime endeavors. He shows executive ability.

Capricorn

Capricorn dominant indicates an individual who is serious, highly organized, and very systematic in the approach to life. He will let very few things pass him without first using these skills. Ambition is highly developed and avidly pursued.

Aquarius

Aquarius dominant indicates an individual who has an abiding interest in science and education, and an instinctive knowledge of human nature. This person will love to discuss theories to the point of argument.

Pisces

Pisces dominant will indicate a very versatile individual whose life seems to have more variety than is average. This individual is sympathetic to a fault and inclined to view things from the point of romance rather than stark reality - the psychic rather than the scientist.

Particular jobs and actions in life are well suited to certain methods of expression. Such jobs and such actions are done best by the individual who has the requisite signs strong by astrodynes.

Houses

The houses indicate environment. They indicate the various areas in the arena of life. When certain of the houses are dominant, certain areas of life are the focus of considerable energy. Because of the power and the planetary urges expressing through the house, an individual is drawn to that area of life.

The house itself is not the active force; it is the planetary energy or energies expressing through the house that activate it. Thus, it is the need for expression of the planetary energies that prompts the individual to seek expression in the environment indicated by the house. The activity of certain environments indicates areas where the individual will find a great portion of his life's energies spent. In keeping with our prior analysis of the signs we will briefly cover what each house's dominance can mean in a chart.

First House

Personal affairs are the most important in the life—those things which relate to the health, the physical body, and to purely personal things. Look for the individual to seek a means of personal expression in most of what he does. Personal concerns will take primary emphasis over the other concerns in life.

Second House

Possessions are very important. The act of obtaining possessions or wealth is perhaps more important than the amount. This house governs both income and outgo, so expression by means of possessions will be important. This house can mean mental and spiritual possessions, too, though it rarely does. Survival is necessary in the physical world, and the second house indicates the means and facility of obtaining those things that help us survive.

Third House

Vocal and literary expression are important, whether incoming via reading and viewing, or outgoing with conversation and writing. While the affairs with neighbors or relatives (all relations but children, mother, and father) can play a strong role in the life, more often writing, study, and conversation are highlighted. In one way or another the events of life will involve these things strongly.

Fourth House

Home environment is important. It colors the life. To a great extent the individual will make a home every place he is in for any length of time. The fourth house also governs real estate, farming, and property. It is possible that much of the life will be spent in the pursuit of these things, according to the physical possibilities. It is a psychic house, governing the end of things. Many strong impressions and instincts govern life's reactions. Where the eighth house governs discarnate entities, and the twelfth house elemental entities, the fourth house indicates the individual's soul and its formative period, as well as intuitions and instincts. Each of these will play a strong part in the life. It is important to note that the fourth house does not show active thought urges prompting instinct. It maps the contact with the environment which evokes a response that stimulates the intuition.

Fifth House

Children—the desire for and care of—can be a strong force in the life. Pleasure and entertainment may be an overwhelming force in the life. As in each other house, the focus on one area usually precludes another facet. Lovemaking looms as a large factor in the consciousness. Hobbies and other forms of relaxation are activities of this house that may assume major proportion in the life.

Sixth House

Work is important. The person is drawn to an environment where he can express the desire to work. Part of this attraction will be association with the people he will have to work with. This house, indicating the method of work, will show the importance of method and its prominence in the consciousness. Whenever there is an opportunity, problems with those in one's employ will become important. Illness will play a strong part, whether personal or from contact with those who are ill. Service is the keyword when this house is dominant.

Seventh House

Marriage will be of prime importance to this individual. In this phase of partnership is included those who are committed to each other and who are caring for the other's needs and responsibilities. It is the need of another who is equal to the individual. When a love affair becomes a stable or more or less permanent part of the life, the other person is shown by the seventh house. Where affections enter not, business partnership is likely to show. But whatever the case, the tendency toward association with another person is strong. The seventh house rules the public in general and open enemies. To the extent that partners are not present in the life, the public and/or open enemies will assume a very important part in the life.

Eighth House

Money of others will be important, and to a large extent the life will be dependent on others' money. Taxes and debts owed and collected can assume importance, especially if the occupation puts one in such a position. If married, dating, or in a partnership, the money of the partner, and in general accounting procedures, will be important. The need to regenerate the life and rejuvenate it will be felt often. This house governs discarnate entities, and when it is dominant it indicates that these entities will contribute much to the success or failure of life. Many events and reactions of life will be traceable to this sensitivity and the results of such contact.

Ninth House

In some manner or another, public expression of opinion is important. Public speaking, teaching, and publishing are all methods that seem attractive. If events have been such as to prevent the foregoing, philosophy in one form or another will occupy one's energies. Dreams will assume an importance and many times will be of considerable value. On the most physical level of this outward expression, long journeys will be prominent, and the experiences gained will be important to development.

Tenth House

Reputation will be a prime factor in the reactions of this individual. Fame, gained by hard work or notoriety, are both expression of the need for reputation. Those people in a position of authority will play an important part in the affairs and events of life. The mother and her influence will do a great deal in molding the life and ideals that will express later as the goals of life. To individuals in positions which allow fewer opportunities for fame or occupation, the mother may play an important role in life.

Eleventh House

The need for friends and their opinion of the individual will occupy a central theme in the person's life. A wide variety of associates—people who are not dear, but who are somewhat close by virtue of repeated association—and acquaintances will contribute much to the success and outlook in life. Hopes are ruled by this house, and it can probably be lumped with the ideals and desires which create our mental enjoyment and satisfaction, just as the opposite house governs the more physical aspects of our pleasure.

Twelfth House

Self-restriction and disappointments have a lasting effect on this individual. These restrictions more often than not come about because of the self-made choices of the individual, who often will wish for both things between which the choice is made. Disappointments come from the restrictions felt. The effect of secret enemies can be considerable. There is a strong desire to keep many feelings and actions secret, although this can be difficult since the house is above the horizon.

Confinement in one manner or another becomes important, whether it is personal confinement or association with occupation, avocation, or everyday affairs which bring contact with confinement. Institutions are a part of this category. Elemental entities and forces are ruled by the twelfth house, and the effect of these can make a considerable impact on the life.

Again, we must indicate that houses must be placed in their proper perspective. The houses do not create the desire for events. Rather, they indicate the environment which will elicit events belonging to that area of life. For example, in the sixth house we talked about method of work being important. What the sixth house accomplishes is to bring the individual into contact with environmental conditions which create a consciousness—or a need—to develop a method or approach to work.

To state the difference more bluntly:

- Planets create a drive from within.
- Houses show environmental forces shaping the needs from without.

Signs show the mean by which either the internal or external environments will express.

Chapter 3

Aspects

*N*ot a great deal can be said about aspects in a general sense, and yet an analysis of the separate factors of astrology would not be complete without considering them. We cannot make a list like we did with planets, signs, and houses. The strength of the aspect depends on its closeness as well as the specific aspect.

In the body of the astrodyne graph where the aspects are listed is where we find our information. It is often found that a strong semisextile (angular house, near perfect) is stronger than a wide conjunction. We all know that a conjunction is innately stronger than a semisextile, but when you wish to know the major aspects affecting the life, we must certainly say that those aspects with the most power will have the most outstanding effects. Further, it will enable the astrologer to sort out in order of importance the aspects to a planet under consideration in each chart. Sun,

Moon, or Mercury opposition Saturn are always feared in a chart. But if the chart contains the aspect with only 1+ astrodyne, it is obviously going to be among the weakest aspects affecting Sun, Moon, or Mercury. Its effect can well be minimized in our assessment of the horoscope.

Another useful aspect of astrodynes, and one highly underrated, is that you can tell which planet will predominate in the aspect. One planet is likely to have more astrodynes than the other. Thus we can find which planet has the stronger influence in the aspect. We find that the chart and its aspects are weighted toward that which is dominant. We must remember that when two planets are in aspect, the sum total of the energy they have to express is available to the aspect. Think of it—exceptionally fine precision would mean taking into account all other aspects to the two planets in question as they created the total planetary energy. Each person is unique!

The harmony of aspects is likewise subject to analysis and will indicate the greatest sources of pleasure and fortune, or of misfortune. Since we have the exact amounts in front of us, we can, when delineating a chart, pick the best combinations of power and harmony that will benefit an individual.

In summary, the greatest probable usefulness of knowing the astrodynes made by each aspect is to put into the proper order of importance each of the aspects made by and to a planet when delineating it. This itself will lend more precision to delineation. The precision of knowing just how strong and what relationship the parts of the chart have to each other is well worth the effort. If, for example, a semisquare was stronger than a conjunction, we'd know that the friction (semisquare) indicated would play a larger part, as would the planet making the aspect, than would the conjunction and the planet making it. Our interpretation would focus more on the friction and less on the prominence (conjunction) and the reading would be more accurate. Without the mathematical results, we would assign the conjunction more power and consequently give our delineation an emphasis which would not match the person's nature as closely as it should.

Chapter 4

Temperament, Disposition, and Health

*T*here are four different things to consider when delineating temperament and disposition. The first and most important item is the *dominant* planet.

The dominant planet indicates the strongest desires in the chart. The temperament is defined as a predominating mood over a long period of time. The strongest planet in a chart will demand outlet more of the time than any other, and its mood will determine the temperament and disposition.

The other three factors are, in order, personality as shown by rising sign and planets in the first house; the mentality as shown by the Moon; and character, which is shown by the Sun. If the Sun or Moon is the dominant planet, then the temperament takes on more of the nature of the character or mentality, respectively.

There is nothing complicated about judging the temperament from the dominant planet. The temperament will be that noted under the analysis of the planets in Chapter 1. The house involved will show what environment has the most effect on the temperament. Whether expression of temperament will help or hinder the individual depends upon the harmony of the planet involved. For example, consider a chart with Jupiter in Capricorn in the second house dominant. As far as the temperament goes, this person will be optimistic, jovial, confident. While inclined to some seriousness and organization in Capricorn, this person will always have faith in his ability to come out on top. Whether it will express as abundance or conceit depends on the harmony. Since the house of personality in this chart is occupied by the Sun in Sagittarius, for one, the Jupiter traits will have an effect on the personality, reinforcing its nature. Because Jupiter is in the second house, it indicates that money and possessions most strongly affect the mood or temperament and stimulate the benevolence or the overconfidence.

Health is shown by the rulers of the first and sixth houses, as well as the Sun for vitality and the Moon for the constitution. Also, any strong and discordant aspects and planets can be factors in disease.

If the Sun is strong by astrodynes, the vitality will be strong. If discordant at the same time, the vitality will be strong, but there will be many difficulties which will put sudden strain on it. If it is sufficiently discordant, the predominance of discord may attract enough difficulties that vitality is permanently impaired (death). Barring such a discordant nature, the metabolism will be active.

If the Moon is strong, the constitution will stand up well, regardless of what comes along. By strong, we mean among the stronger in the chart. You can't draw a line and say the first three, four, or five planets in the list are strong. Each chart will show a distribution which will suggest what is strength, what is lack of it, and what is moderate.

If the Sun or Moon is weak, there is more chance of difficulty, for there is not as much energy available to bolster the vitality or the constitution. If either is weak but harmonious, the good fortune may—just may—carry the individual through. There never will be an exceptionally strong constitution or vitality, though; just good fortune such as the amount of energy is. If Sun and Moon are weak, and the harmony is not great, they may break down under the first great strain brought by progressions or events. Strong discordant aspects, and in a more general way, strongly discordant planets, indicate the nature of health difficulties to look for.

For instance, Mercury strong and discordant, or weak and discordant, will be subject to nervous difficulties, mental error and damage to nerves, mental breakdown, and so on. A complete breakdown of each planet is in the Brotherhood of Light courses *Delineating the Horoscope* and *Stellar Healing*. Dietary aid may be found in *Personal Alchemy*.

25

What is important to us here is the manner in which astrodynes can contribute to health analysis. Let us enumerate the ways.

1. The strength of the planets indicates the activity and the ability to withstand illness.

2. The harmony (or its lack) indicates which desires will attract discord, and the nature of it. Here again the strength of the aspect and the amount of this discord will determine which things are most likely to occur.

3. Sign strength and harmony are useful to indicate areas of difficulty in regard to body location.

Be careful not to confuse planet activity and its need for a suitable outlet. The author, for instance, is constantly banging his knee. Capricorn rules the knees, and no planets are in Capricorn, and its ruler is the second weakest and most discordant planet in the chart. These incidents are in response to Mars, not in response to Capricorn stimulation. Why the knees? Weak and afflicted Capricorn. Anyone who knows the stature of the author knows that his legs do not fit well into the world about him, and the necessity of expressing the Mars takes its most easily available outlet. The essential factor is an outlet for Mars.

Another example. Venus rules the venous blood system. If a vein were to "pop," that would involve Venus. Which part of the body might be determined by which sign was weakest, or most discordant.

Another way of saying it is, astrology doesn't predict; it just shows what energies are guaranteed to be stimulating you. Taking into account resistance of the environment is absolutely necessary in ascertaining a person's reactions. It is too bad that we haven't any mathematical means at present of ascertaining the amount of resistance the environment offers.

Chapter 5

Vocational Analysis

*T*here are two different approaches to vocational analysis: one concentrating on ability, the other concentrating on luck—or fortune—with the job. In either case, astrodynes are indispensable.

The dominant planet indicates the capabilities in the chart that are most easily tapped. The second and third strongest indicate capabilities that are next in strength. Those capabilities which have the most power in the makeup *should* be capitalized upon when choosing an occupation. Success today is based upon the same things it always has been: ability and application. With your strongest abilities at work you can have the greatest chance of making a success. If the dominant planet is discordant (which is most often true), then there may be some unpleasant things associated with it. But I know of no famous person today—one whose success was more than a flash in the

29

pan—who has not worked through difficulties and in so doing become better able to handle growing success.

There are those who emphasize choosing an occupation according to the most harmonious planet, so that the fortune involved will be the best possible. Unfortunately, the planet which is selected may be weak, so that the desires of the individual will be strong in other directions.

If the dominant planet has a great deal of discord, there are still likely to be harmonious aspects to this planet. A look at the astrodyne graph will tell us which aspect will yield the most harmony to the dominant planet. If the planet thus aspected and the house it is in are worked into the occupation, such association will allow for little else but harmony.

One thing is certain: People are happiest doing something they can do well and that is attractive to them. If they are not following thei dominant abilities, these abilities and desires will tear at them until satisfied.

Sometimes it is not always possible for the dominant planet to be utilized fully. If the second dominant planet can be developed, a certain amount of satisfaction can be attained.

In order to fully indicate vocational selection, the temperament of the individual must be taken into account. This again is chiefly determined by the dominant planet and, to a lesser degree, by the Ascendant and planets in the first house. The strongest influence in the chart thus indicates that the abilities and the temperament to utilize them are one and the same.

The strength of the house has a great deal of significance. Because many occupations require association with a particular environment, a strong house will create the frequent contact with the specific environment, causing a natural inclination toward the vocation. Before the advent of astrodynes, prominence was a speculative, or at best, educated guess analysis. Now we have at our fingertips in the astrodyne graph which houses are strongest. This, with the planets' strength, will give us a good clue to the potential vocations to be followed. As an instance, doctors usually have Mars and Jupiter prominent, as well as the sixth and twelfth houses. Mars is for surgery and healing, and Jupiter for the professional status and the study necessary. A person with a dominant sixth house is brought naturally into contact with illness and surroundings where there is illness, and with a dominant twelfth house, the environment of institutions and confinement (which indicates hospitals).

Space does not permit listing each vocation researched and what planets need to be active for each. Suffice it to say here that if the strong planets in the chart, as well as the houses, are those necessary for a specific occupation, guidance should be given accordingly. Those who wish to know which planets need to be strong should obtain the Church of Light *Astrological Research and Reference Cyclopedia* (two volumes). This is a reprint of the original publication of Church of Light research by Elbert Benjamine, published and copyrighted by the Church of Light. It is the only complete and authentic place it can be found. Also a great help is the *Outline of Astrological Vocational Analysis* compiled by Mathilda Shepard, which is also published and copyrighted by the Church of Light. In it will be found not only the various factors necessary to vocational selection, but which factors can be found by astrodynes. For the purposes of this book, we give some points to help in vocational analysis. These pointers will give some much needed additional insight into the problems of vocational selection, and when combined with the constants found by research, should give the necessary tools for vocational guidance.

Sun

If the Sun is strong the job must contain opportunity for leadership or to be heading up something—even if it is head of a one-man department. While it is true that the Sun inclines to managers and politics, etc., it is not possible for every Sun dominant to rise supreme in these areas. What is important is that the person get an occupation where his sense of importance is emphasized. Thus, a woman with a strong Sun might do well as an executive secretary. Why this analysis with the Sun? Because this job offers the possibility of attaining importance to the employer and becoming "indispensable."

Moon

If the Moon is strong, the job should contain the opportunity to work with the public. A job where understanding and sympathy can be applied and where the mental capabilities can be exercised is important. It is not especially pertinent any more to indicate waiters, clerks, and "common" occupations, for many occupations deal with everyday people. Thus a lawyer could have a dominant Moon—especially the one who donates help to such things as "public assistance."

Mercury

If Mercury is strong, a job with writing, calculation, keen perception, or reading is a must. The person with Mercury strong must have the opportunity to express his thinking processes. Be careful not to stereotype occupations. The important thing is to fit the abilities of the strong planet to a job. Thus, a clergyman might have a dominant Mercury, for he might be inclined to writing on religion, or perhaps specially gifted with the ability to express from the pulpit.

Venus

If Venus is strong, a job that is not hard or dirty is generally indicated. A job that calls for artistic expression and mental creativity is necessary. A job that allows the individual to create or arrange beauty is important. Again, it is the ability to somehow express a strong desire that is important. A manager could have a dominant Venus, especially if managing a modeling agency or interior decorating firm, or maybe a textile plant—just so there is the opportunity to help create and make the artistic or beautiful.

Mars

If Mars is strong, the job should contain the possibility of physical work and effort. This is not paramount. What is especially important to Mars is that there be opportunities to express initiative, to find out what resistance there is to the job and overcome it. Thus, a carpenter, a troubleshooter, a pottery maker, or an athlete may have Mars strong—just as long as there is the chance to overcome obstacles, especially those of a physical nature. Activity is a must, or the Mars will revolt.

Jupiter

If Jupiter is strong, salesmanship and professional ethics are important factors. When Jupiter is strong the occupation must contain the opportunity to cater to those who have influence, to those whose business is of a high caliber of education. It must offer the person the opportunity to sell himself, an idea, product, or company. Thus, a personnel director could fit the bill with a strong Jupiter in that he would have a chance to select people for the company. Not everyone can be a doctor or lawyer or top-notch salesman, per se, with Jupiter prominent. But put them in a job where these things are available.

Saturn

If Saturn is dominant, organization and system must be available—no, necessary, for the individual. While there is a strong attraction for things of the earth, such as real estate, mining, and farming, there are many, many people with a strong Saturn that are not interested in them due to conditioning. What is needed is a job with a systematic approach, or one where organization is needed. Responsibility and hard work will be natural to a strong Saturn. Thus, it is possible for a caterer to have a dominant Saturn, for he will arrange and plan dining and party events, and his success will depend upon the degree of system and organization he has accomplished.

Uranus

If Uranus is strong, originality, inventiveness, and ingenuity must be available. Uranus is happiest when it has a chance to take an old method or ideas and do something new. Working with people is a must, especially in a capacity where his knowledge of human nature can get a chance to exercise itself. The occupation must be one that keeps the individual changing.

Neptune

If Neptune is strong, a job without dirty tasks, one that allows for imagination and perhaps a bit of promoting is important. The job should allow for a certain level of privacy—being around large numbers of people does not set well with Neptune. Any job that will allow for dramatization will go far in satisfying this individual. Salesman, writer, composer—these are some areas Neptune can be comfortable in.

Pluto

If Pluto is strong, the necessity of working with groups of people will be evident. There is also a tendency to become involved with things relating to high frequency energies, such as television. Any mass medium where people can be swayed in large numbers is governed in part at least by Pluto. In the more average life, Pluto will make cooperation or its bad brother coercion an essential part of the occupation. The individual will not be happy if there is not an opportunity to work with others, either voluntarily or against their will. The job must be one where mass production methods can be utilized, and where a high degree of specialization may be attained. Pluto strong will be primarily interested in finding an area of specialization and developing as fully as the capabilities allow. A television repairman could fit Pluto as well as Henry Ford.

Midheaven and Ascendant

We should say something here about the Midheaven and the Ascendant. These two points are neutral and receptive. They depend upon aspects to them to stimulate them into activity. The more aspects, and the stronger the aspects are, the more activity the Midheaven and Ascendant show. Their nature is colored by the aspects. They have a function to perform, which they do when activated.

The Midheaven relates to the job—at least the job desired, if not the type of superiors and their reaction to him and he to them. Aspects to the Midheaven create the tendency to broadcast the characteristics of the aspecting planet to as wide a segment of life as possible. If the Midheaven is stronger than anything, we still look to the strongest planet as the dominant planet; but on the other hand, we note that honor, reputation, and job receive the greatest amount of stimulation in the chart, and the individual's greatest share of energy in his life will be in the pursuit of these things.

The Ascendant represents the ground line over which the physical being is polarized. Aspects to it directly affect the body and personality. When the Ascendant is strongest, it indicates that the personality expression, personal affairs, and the physical body get more attention than does anything else in the chart. It must be remembered that only because the Ascendant has many aspects stimulating it to action, does it exercise such a strong effect on the person.

Chapter 6

Compatibility

*T*he rules for ascertaining compatibility insofar as physical magnetism, mental outlook, and spiritual outlook are the same as found in the Brotherhood of Light course, *Delineating the Horoscope*. These are dependent on the Ascendant, Moon, and Sun, and the signs they are in. Our discussion here is to look at some of the ways in which astrodynes can aid in determining compatibility. Many times they show why two people didn't get along that should have seemed to, and vice versa.

Sun sign, Moon sign, and Ascendant were all compatible, but it was all the way to the divorce court. What went wrong? In one chart the dominant planet is Saturn; in the other, it is Mars. The dominant Saturn never will reconcile (unless by deliberate and strong effort) to the impulsiveness of Mars. The dominant Mars never will understand the slow methodical way of Saturn. The difference builds up, until @%+&!???

Sun signs in the same triplicity and a Moon that matches the other's Ascendant are compatible. The people feel comfortable in each other's presence, yet the relationship is about to blow. One partner has a very strong Venus; the other has a weak Venus. The first individual wishes to express a great deal of affection and craves it in return. The person with the weak Venus neither needs much nor understands the constant need of the other partner.

If the same situation existed where Mars was strong in the chart where Venus was weak, there is a good chance that there would be a common ground. This common ground could be the lovemaking. The Mars impulse is toward sex; Venus is toward the expression of love. The dominant Venus might not get just affection. But the person with the weak Venus and Mars prominent would desire an active sex life during which the attention and love paid the person with the dominant Venus would suffice. Not that this situation would be completely fulfilling to either (a dominant Mars would prefer an equally martial partner in love), but it might be adequate enough for a good partnership.

To a similar degree, partnerships and associations of a less personal nature are still subject to the same considerations. Impulsive Mars is not likely to want to understand or appreciate methodical Saturn. These principles are pertinent on all levels of association. Another thought to consider: When two people have the same planet dominant, and both have it discordant, compatibility may be strained by both expressing the discordant side of what are similar natures. On the other hand, given sufficient energy, a harmonious planet in the chart of one person may do much to counteract the discord of another's. Do not confuse this with the reaction of two planets in the same degree between two charts. What this means is that where it comes to expressing the specific urges shown by a planet in one chart, the harmony will prompt an approach that may cause the possessor of the discordant planets to react more favorably when faced with the first person's more harmonious action!

It is impossible, even with astrodynes, to advise all of the shadings possible. Even in the case of both people having the same planet dominant and discordant, each could have a harmonious aspect between the dominant planet and the ruler of the seventh house (partners), in which case they would react favorably toward each other and find common ground in facing the discords of the dominant planet together. Even astrodynes won't synthesize a chart or draw the conclusions in a chart based on all pertinent facts. This must still be done by an astrologer.

Another area is that of houses. When the strength of houses varies too much, there is not going to be much common ground of expression. We cannot say that such a house in this chart has more astrodynes than in that chart. Rather, this judgment must be rendered by noting that a particular house in this chart is stronger in relation to the rest of them than is the same house in that chart in relation to the rest of the houses in that chart. When there is not similar power in the same houses between charts, that means that each person will be drawn to different environments than the other. This can cause difficulty when the interests of one never coincide with those of the other.

This same reasoning can be applied to signs. The analysis of Sun, Moon, and Ascendant signs teaches us which signs are antagonistic and which are concordant. When the dominant signs are antagonistic to each other, it will take a powerful number of other indications for good not to cause problems. We can extend this, in a more general way, to the triplicities, qualities, societies, and trinities of houses. A heavily fixed person will find difficulty with a heavily mutable or movable person, and vice versa. Two planets within a degree of each other in a chart can make a powerful reaction, one which will attempt to defy other indications at least during the first stagesof association. But at least we can determine with exactness the areas of difficulty and prepare to handle them.

As a quick rule of thumb, associations with others can be grouped as follows in order of the strength of attachment:

- Strongest attraction: a planet in one chart conjunct a planet in another *within one degree only*.
- Sun, Moon, and Ascendant compatible.
- Planets in the same signs.
- Planets in concordant signs (fire, air, etc.).
- No similarity.

Chapter 7

Progressions

*B*efore bringing this section to a close, we should mention briefly the matter of progressions. When the astrodynes of progressions are done, there is still some question about what to do with them. If you do not feel that astrodynes of progressions have been explained adequately, you should obtain *Astrodyne Manual* by Elbert Benjamine, which goes into this phase in considerable detail.

By this time it would serve little purpose to go into a list by planet of what to expect if such and such is extremely strong by progression. The interpretation of the planets is the same as we have been using. The only thing we can add in this chapter is the manner in which we look at the astrodynes.

When we get through calculating the astrodynes of progressions, we are working with significantly increased amounts of power. Because of this it begins to boggle the mind as to what it means. I believe that the best way to make sense of it is to find the percentage of increase of the power. To do this, divide the natal power into the progressed power and multiply by 100 to get a percentage. Increased to 200 percent would indicate doubled strength, etc. In this manner we can see how much increase relative to the natal has occurred. The greater the percentage, the greater the effect. But remember, a planet with six times as much power as it had, that is weak in the natal chart, may not be as strong as a planet strong in the natal chart that has increased two and a half times.

This means you will notice a remarkable increase in manifestation of the weaker natal planet, but that it still won't be as strong as that of the progressed planet. Yet, as much stronger as it is, it will seem more eventful than that which had come to be expected from the natal chart before stimulation.

All of the interpretation holds true with the progressed planets. Strong aspects will indicate some of the predominating temperamental transits for the period of time of the aspect(s). Temporary vocational considerations and events are shown. Also it shows those temporary energies which strongly draw two people together for the duration of the aspect. Whatever the case, the amount of strength and the amount of increase will give us a better view of those progressed energies more strongly affecting us.

Incidentally, when trying to figure percentages of harmony, the same procedure as with power does not work. Harmony is on a plus and minus basis. Unless both the natal harmony and the amount of progressed harmony are the same sign (plus or minus), you can't divide the two. If they are of different signs (plus or minus), add the two amounts together and divide the natal amount into this total to get the increase or decrease of harmony. The answer multiplied by 100 gives the percentage.

Astrodynes do not help predict exact events. We know which energies are most insistent, but astrology cannot predict exact events. It can only show the possibilities inherent in a situation, and imply which possibilities are most available in a given environment. Not even astrodynes can help with this judgment. Analysis, judgment, and discrimination—these are the function of the astrologer using all the tools available to help him weigh all the facts in their proper relationship.

Chapter 8

Temperament

*I*n Chapter 4 we covered the effects of a dominant planet on temperament and disposition, which were given specifically. In this chapter we cover just briefly the outstanding traits in a couple of charts and see how the astrodynes indicate the situation.

Charts 1 and 2

Charts 1 and 2 are husband and wife, respectively. His outstanding characteristic—that which is consistently present—may best be summed up in the fact he is a perfect host. He will have equal time for the least person in a room as he will have for the most important. His dominant planet is the Sun, whose best qualities are kindness and consideration. Leo is the dominant sign, giving him the impetus to be the center of a group, a characteristic which his truly regal carriage and look demand.

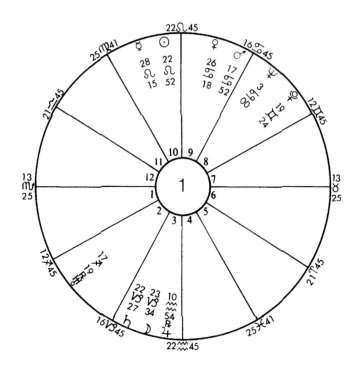

Planets — Part I			Signs -- Part II			Houses — Part III		
☉	102.75	+ 5.53	♈	19.86	- 5.63	1	61.51	- 4.63
☽	42.93	-11.70	♉	13.31	- 4.31	2	50.99	+ 2.27
☿	69.72	+ 6.08	♊	89.69	+ 8.65	3	117.50	-41.41
♀	26.62	- 8.62	♋	114.80	-26.94	4	39.66	- 4.29
♂	39.72	-11.25	♌	309.30	+20.25	5	11.31	- .39
♃	18.33	- .34	♍	34.86	+ 3.04	6	19.86	- 5.63
♄	37.49	-19.56	♎	13.31	- 4.31	7	13.31	- 4.31
♅	41.82	+ 2.44	♏	61.51	- 4.63	8	116.68	+ 7.43
♆	26.99	- 1.22	♐	50.99	+ 2.27	9	87.81	-25.72
♇	54.83	+ 5.61	♑	99.17	-41.07	10	309.30	+20.25
MC	85.45	+ 5.87	♒	57.99	- 4.63	11	34.86	+ 3.04
ASC	37.87	- 3.22	♓	11.31	- .39	12	13.31	- 4.31
Total			Total			Total		

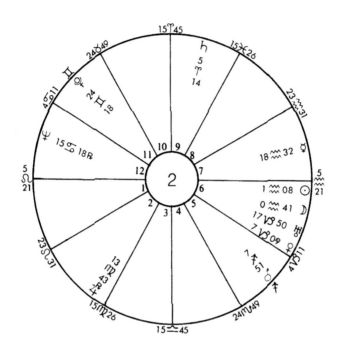

Planets — Part I   Signs — Part II   Houses — Part III

Planets — Part I			Signs — Part II			Houses — Part III		
☉	28.97	- 4.62	♈	96.85	-10.75	1	64.82	- .28
☽	48.29	- 5.33	♉	16.53	+ .37	2	49.96	+15.22
☿	33.47	+10.27	♊	35.80	+12.25	3	16.74	+ 5.14
♀	33.05	+ .74	♋	59.67	-11.48	4	16.53	+ .37
♂	30.41	+ 7.08	♌	79.30	- 2.59	5	53.25	+15.66
♃	35.47	+17.51	♍	52.21	+22.67	6	176.51	-10.36
♄	38.00	- 2.32	♎	16.53	+ .37	7	54.77	+ 9.69
♅	47.20	+ .01	♏	14.47	+ 4.19	8	21.30	- .58
♆	35.52	- 8.81	♐	39.28	+15.85	9	55.75	- .14
♇	27.43	+ 9.68	♑	99.25	- .41	10	58.85	- 8.43
MC	43.64	-11.97	♒	153.33	- .84	11	52.33	+12.62
ASC	50.33	+ 2.03	♓	17.25	+ 2.18	12	59.67	-11.48
Total	451.78	+14.29	Total			Total		

47

Her outstanding characteristics are the need to be the center of attention and to constantly be the first to propose some new interest, usually philosophical, to which she has to win over all acquaintances. The center of attention would normally be an outlet of the Sun—the drive for significance. However, the Sun is next to the weakest thing in the chart. Notice that the Ascendant in Leo is the strongest thing in her chart. So it is the Leo characteristics expressing through personality that bring the need for the center of attention.

Therefore, in delineating this chart, to determine what things affect this need for attention, we would be more interested in the aspects to the Ascendant and less so for the aspects to the Sun. Notice also that the Moon is in the originality decanate of Aquarius and Uranus is next strongest, which would give the tendency to embrace new things and constant change.

Charts 3 and 4

Chart 3 has Neptune dominant. This person, whose financial policy (Neptune in the second house) of buying what was desired first and paying bills second caused considerable difficulty, was strongly attracted to music. He has never had the get up and go to go far with it.

Chart 4 is the chart of a religious fanatic whose personality characteristics include a perverted love of bad odors as well as the conviction she is being hounded by the spirit of Ezekiel. This chart leaves one baffled from the dominant planet viewpoint. The Ascendant and the Midheaven are the most powerful, indicating a negative or receptive nature to begin with. Saturn is the strongest planet, with

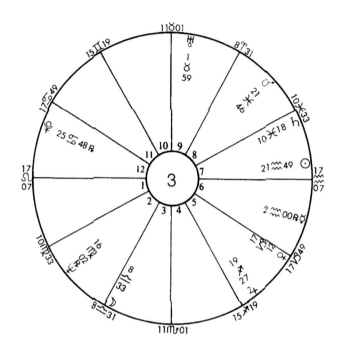

Planets — Part I			Signs — Part II			Houses — Part III		
☉	37.31	−11.34	♈	15.56	+ .72	1	64.97	− 5.31
☽	15.50	− 2.19	♉	84.00	+ 7.83	2	66.29	−19.74
☿	27.55	−12.01	♊	13.78	− 6.01	3	28.59	+11.06
♀	26.17	+26.50	♋	32.77	−10.10	4	14.04	− 1.89
♂	31.12	+ 1.44	♌	64.97	− 5.31	5	79.51	+49.00
♃	35.56	+15.00	♍	66.29	−19.74	6	48.30	−19.95
♄	42.50	−15.88	♎	28.59	+11.06	7	96.69	−34.14
♅	25.01	−11.80	♏	14.04	− 1.89	8	53.14	− .45
♆	52.51	−13.73	♐	53;34	+22;50	9	40.57	−11.08
♇	25.02	− 9.00	♑	47.42	+18.56	10	58.99	+19.63
MC	45.90	+ 6.38	♒	81.74	−30.27	11	13.78	− 6.01
ASC	46.31	+ .36	♓	95.64	−14.12	12	32.77	−10.10
Total			Total			Total		

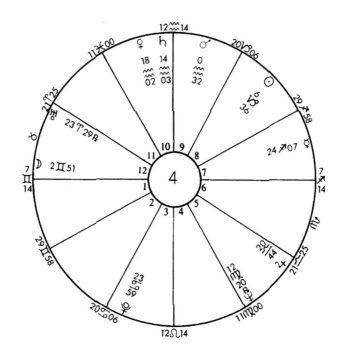

Planets — Part I

			Signs — Part II			Houses — Part III		
☉	39.40	+ 3.30	♈	51.21	+12.49	1	84.07	+ .95
☽	23.58	+ 4.20	♉	10.01	+ 3.41	2	21.90	+ 5.99
☿	43.80	+11.97	♊	129.55	+11.13	3	47.24	-11.87
♀	40.02	+13.62	♋	47.24	-11.87	4	19.70	+ 1.65
♂	28.73	+ 5.89	♌	19.70	+ 1.65	5	87.05	+23.19
♃	41.04	+21.73	♍	46.01	+ 1.76	6	28.04	+ 8.85
♄	47.12	- 4.04	♎	61.05	+28.59	7	64.32	+22.84
♅	36.84	+ 9.54	♏	8.03	- 2.02	8	59.92	+14.17
♆	24.11	- 4.23	♐	84.84	+33.70	9	52.29	+ 3.87
♇	35.45	-13.97	♑	31.48	+ 1.28	10	159.91	+12.23
MC	51.78	+ 1.27	♒	188.14	+19.49	11	16.29	+ 4.38
ASC	62.17	- 5.04	♓	16.29	+ 4.38	12	84.80	+20.10
Total			Total			Total		

Mercury, Venus, and Jupiter close by. It is interesting to note that the planets are grouped closely in power, and that eight of the twelve are harmonious. Such harmony indicates one for whom things are being constantly smoothed out. When the aspects are viewed, the main strong aspects involve Jupiter (religious) opposing Uranus (unusual, the reformer) and Uranus square Pluto (perversion). Of any other strong aspects, the ones to Mercury in the seventh house conciliating the opposition are the others. This indicates how the husband provides escape for the native as he helps to "keep the lid on" her activities. Here also is a case where the value of environment and conditioning are important, for her two daughters are "sexually perverted;" the individual's sisters are likewise. The environment offered easy opportunity for these traits to occur. Still, Saturn dominant and afflicted leans to perverted desires. In every case the dominant planet will show the temperament.

Chapter 9

Vocational Selection

*V*ocational selection is not a simple matter of picking a pro-
fession from among those generally associated with a
planet. While it is true sometimes, more often than not the vocation is apart from the fields generally indicated by a planet.
We've said this before, and in a couple of charts we will see this
statement bear truth.

What happens is that the dominant planets indicate the
specific qualities and abilities used in the occupation.
Thus, a managerial person (Sun ability) may be a manager
in electronics, in wearing apparel, or a sales manager.
And in the field of sales, there are infinite varieties of
products, etc.

Another example is that the Sun rules politicians and jobs
involving political people and actions. Yet many politicians do not have dominant Suns.

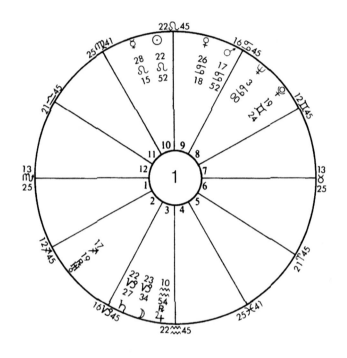

Planets — Part I			Signs -- Part II			Houses — Part III		
☉	102.75	+ 5.53	♈	19.86	- 5.63	1	61.51	- 4.63
☽	42.93	-11.70	♉	13.31	- 4.31	2	50.99	+ 2.27
☿	69.72	+ 6.08	♊	89.69	+ 8.65	3	117.50	-41.41
♀	26.62	- 8.62	♋	114.80	-26.94	4	39.66	- 4.29
♂	39.72	-11.25	♌	309.30	+20.25	5	11.31	- .39
♃	18.33	- .34	♍	34.86	+ 3.04	6	19.86	- 5.63
♄	37.49	-19.56	♎	13.31	- 4.31	7	13.31	- 4.31
♅	41.82	+ 2.44	♏	61.51	- 4.63	8	116.68	+ 7.43
♆	26.99	- 1.22	♐	50.99	+ 2.27	9	87.81	-25.72
♇	54.83	+ 5.61	♑	99.17	-41.07	10	309.30	+20.25
MC	85.45	+ 5.87	♒	57.99	- 4.63	11	34.86	+ 3.04
ASC	37.87	- 3.22	♓	11.31	- .39	12	13.31	- 4.31
Total			Total			Total		

Chart 1

Chart 1 is a salesman. What is the planet of salesmen? Jupiter, of course. Wrong in this chart! Jupiter is the weakest planet by far. Under the usual rules of vocational selection it is unlikely that we would suggest being a salesman. Yet he is successful. Let us analyze the situation further. Jupiter usually indicates the temperament that finds selling easy, and obtains the patronage needed. When we look at the chart of this man, we find a dominant Sun, seven minutes from perfect conjunction to the Midheaven, both in Leo. Leo is overwhelmingly dominant among the signs. Leo is considered the natural salesman, and the drive for significance is located there. The tenth house is the dominant house and it rules superiors. The Sun is harmonious, showing good relations with these. As a matter of course, the merchandise he sells relies very little upon patronage. He sells legal calendars and books. These are necessary items to lawyers and judges, and sales rely less upon the patronage of the customers than upon convincing the customer of their contribution to the lawyer's successful practice. He was a chiropractor but quit because he believed in the adage, "physician, heal thyself," and he couldn't. The necessity here was to do something worthwhile that would satisfy his self-esteem and sense of worth.

Chart 5

Chart 5, Albert Einstein, provides us with an interesting insight into what made the man what he was. Traditionally, aspects to Mercury and/or the Moon from Mars are supposed to confer mathematical ability. Einstein had both: a semisquare of Mars and Moon, and a weak sextile

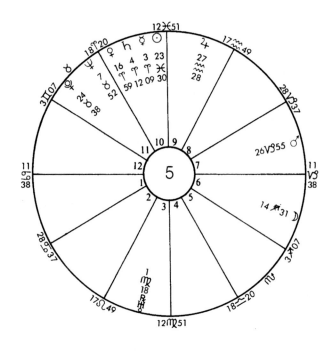

Planets — Part I			Signs — Part II			Houses – Part III		
☉	48.97	+ 5.16	♈	242.35	-25.80	1	59.39	- 6.52
☽	27.78	- 4.94	♉	77.45	+13.38	2	13.89	- 2.47
☿	74.19	- 9.86	♊	37.10	- 4.43	3	46.32	- 3.68
♀	53.08	+ 1.26	♋	73.28	- 8.99	4	37.10	- 4.93
♂	63.98	+ 4.13	♌	24.49	+ 2.58	5	41.90	+ 4.14
♃	30.45	- 1.61	♍	58.93	-11.19	6	43.01	- 5.75
♄	75.59	-23.04	♎	29.04	+ 2.52	7	106.78	- 3.62
♅	21.83	- 6.26	♏	12.86	+ 1.15	8	37.80	-15.30
♆	29.08	+ 7.05	♐	43.01	- 9.52	9	54.81	- 8.94
♇	33.85	+ 5.07	♑	144.57	-15.14	10	315.23	-24.44
MC	43.01	- 3.08	♒	54.81	- 8.94	11	111.94	+15.45
ASC	45.50	- 4.05	♓	107.37	+ 3.44	12	37.10	- 4.03
Total			Total			Total		

of Mercury to Mars. Mercury was very strongly parallel Mars. Interestingly, Mars in the seventh house and Mercury in the tenth house would likely produce an accountant or an actuary. The astrodynes show, however, that Saturn is the dominant planet, with Mercury second a bare hair off the pace. Mercury so strong shows the need for thinking, perception, and calculation. Saturn, also in the tenth house, gives us a key to what really directed him toward his success. Saturn dominant wants organization and system above all. Not satisfied with available explanations and their data, he directed his efforts toward a more orderly and organized concept of the universe and its laws. Perhaps this is why he was considered a flop at everyday arithmetic. His mathematics (Mercury) was a tool by which he satisfied his strongest drive, a more systematic and unified (Saturn) theory of universal relationships.

Chart 6

Chart 6, Walt Disney, offers another interesting picture. He has the most planetary power I have ever seen in one chart: 896 astrodynes. Here, too, is Saturn dominant, followed closely by Sun and Uranus. Clearly the major driving force was that of system and organization. Pride and originality were close behind. The pride and originality surely need no explanation in regard to his fame. No one who has visited Disneyland or Disneyworld can ever doubt the guiding Saturn. With Saturn in the first house, he would ever have been striving with ambition to create for a wide number of people an expression of those personal feelings he had.

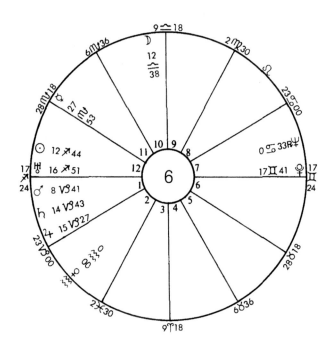

Planets — Part I			Signs — Part II			Houses — Part III		
☉	94.78	+ 8.57	♈	23.55	-13.90	1	401.02	-36.85
☽	81.18	-13.42	♉	75.77	+17.99	2	150.74	- 9.16
☿	29.70	- 2.05	♊	66.94	-22.75	3	40.89	+ 4.98
♀	75.77	+17.99	♋	104.65	-11.79	4	23.55	-13.90
♂	47.10	-27.80	♌	23.69	+ 2.14	5	37.89	+ 9.00
♃	99.49	+25.01	♍	14.85	- 1.03	6	37.89	+ 9.00
♄	101.22	-42.75	♎	172.11	-21.55	7	131.00	-27.83
♅	93.70	- 3.34	♏	79.30	-26.81	8	64.28	- 4.57
♆	64.06	- 5.08	♐	341.69	+17.74	9	14.85	- 1.03
♇	52.09	-21.72	♑	298.42	-66.92	10	172.11	-21.55
MC	53.04	-17.13	♒	100.13	+12.22	11	54.50	-14.43
ASC	103.46	- 3.82	♓	40.89	+ 4.98	12	213.28	- 7.15
Total	895.59	-85.54	Total			Total		

Chart 7

In Chart 7, Ronald Reagan, we have a man who has worn two hats reasonably successfully. In his chart the Midheaven is strongest. This supplies the activity regarding fame and recognition. His dominant planet is Neptune. Neptune governs the dramatic arts and the film industry. With these thought cells being strongest, it is easy to see why his first career was acting. In addition, a scientific astrologer, finding Neptune in the eighth house, might have even suspected a promoter. But acting fits the abilities well. The Sun, considered so necessary to politicians, is weak in the chart. This would lead us to puzzle a little why he is a politician. Considering the dominant Neptune and weak Sun, it would seem apparent that he has some ideal he is trying to attain. This fact would explain why he has made some moves uncharacteristic of the "professional politician." If he continues in politics, it will be because he sees a goal he wants to attain for the office he holds. But he is not as thick-skinned as some people would have us think.

These are some examples of vocations and the charts belonging to the people practicing them. To find an outlet where the greatest exercise of a person's indicated ability or abilities may be used is the prime purpose of the astrologer giving vocational guidance. This area of life is important to people and demands the utmost discrimination to find the most useful job.

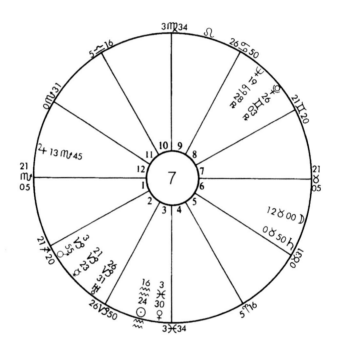

Planets — Part I | Signs — Part II | Houses — Part III

☉	28.31	-14.09	♈	16.39	+ 5.84	1	61.58	+ 8.92
☽	36.28	- 7.24	♉	99.84	- 9.26	2	137.41	- 2.34
☿	47.42	- 7.40	♊	47.69	- 8.55	3	85.28	-16.75
♀	32.54	- 1.42	♋	70.38	- 7.50	4	21.49	- 1.65
♂	32.78	+11.68	♌	7.08	- 3.52	5	16.39	+ 5.84
♃	33.72	+ .57	♍	78.39	- 6.45	6	83.57	- 8.55
♄	31.02	- .60	♎	16.27	- .71	7	16.27	- .71
♅	40.35	- 6.90	♏	109.50	+11.20	8	99.93	-12.43
♆	52.24	- 3.88	♐	16.86	+ .28	9	25.22	- 7.14
♇	23.98	- 4.85	♑	136.06	- 2.92	10	78.39	- 6.45
MC	54.68	- 2.75	♒	37.23	-15.03	11	16.27	- .71
ASC	47.39	+ 7.22	♓	54.03	- 3.07	12	47.91	+ 2.28
Total	460.71	-29.66	Total			Total		

Chapter 10

Compatibility

*T*his chapter includes two examples of compatibility, using three charts previously discussed and another who is the husband of a woman in a previous example.

Charts 8 and 3

Charts 8 and 3 are the charts of husband and wife. Their marriage has been marred by a number of difficulties external to the marriage itself, some that have been rough. Still it seems to have survived well, and we ought to see why.

His dominant planet is Neptune. This is in line with his general notions about life. Neptune inclines to music, and he is a dedicated music lover. Her dominant planet is Venus, followed by Mars, Neptune, and Moon. Venus, Neptune, and Moon give her an interest in music, and she does

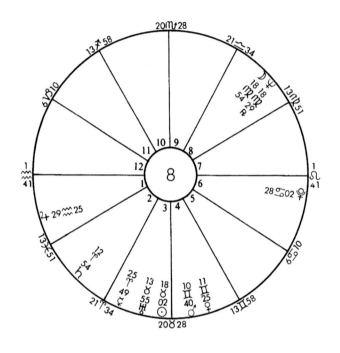

Planets — Part I   Signs — Part II   Houses — Part III

☉	44.27	+ 7.11	♈	78.01	-11.75	1	69.71	- 6.29
☽	50.04	+11.71	♉	107.67	+21.01	2	38.52	+ 5.31
☿	30.48	- 9.16	♊	128.54	-10.86	3	135.80	+ 7.21
♀	59.00	+ 1.49	♋	66.10	-10.22	4	142.80	- 5.53
♂	54.30	-7.77	♌	22.14	+ 3.56	5	15.24	- 4.58
♃	22.06	+ 4.96	♍	115.77	+18.21	6	66.10	-10.22
♄	20.38	+ 1.30	♎	29.50	+ .75	7	22.14	+ 3.56
♅	33.90	+13.15	♏	71.01	- 8.95	8	115.77	+18.21
♆	50.49	+11.08	♐	11.03	+ 2.48	9	29.50	+ .75
♇	41.08	-16.08	♑	10.19	+ .65	10	71.01	- 8.95
MC	47.09	- 3.13	♒	69.71	- 6.29	11	11.03	+ 2.48
ASC	34.08	-14.86	♓	18.14	+ 4.01	12	10.19	+ .65
Total			Total			Total		

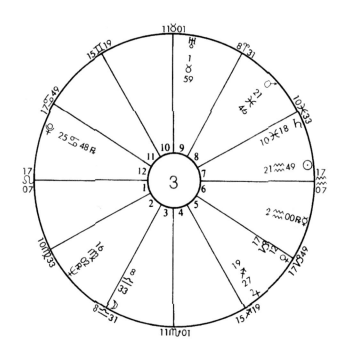

Planets — Part I			Signs — Part II			Houses — Part III		
☉	37.31	-11.34	♈	15.56	+ .72	1	64.97	- 5.31
☽	15.50	- 2.19	♉	84.00	+ 7.83	2	66.29	-19.74
☿	27.55	-12.01	♊	13.78	- 6.01	3	28.59	+11.06
♀	26.17	+26.50	♋	32.77	-10.10	4	14.04	- 1.89
♂	31.12	+ 1.44	♌	64.97	- 5.31	5	79.51	+49.00
♃	35.56	+15.00	♍	66.29	-19.74	6	48.30	-19.95
♄	42.50	-15.88	♎	28.59	+11.06	7	96.69	-34.14
♅	25.01	-11.80	♏	14.04	- 1.89	8	53.14	- .45
♆	52.51	-13.73	♐	53.34	+22.50	9	40.57	-11.08
♇	25.02	- 9.00	♑	47.42	+18.56	10	58.99	+19.63
MC	45.90	+ 6.38	♒	81.74	-30.27	11	13.78	- 6.01
ASC	46.31	+ .36	♓	95.64	-14.12	12	32.77	-10.10
Total			Total			Total		

share the intense like of music. With Mars strong she is more the performer than he, though he seems to have more of a "feel" for it.

They share four departments of life occupied. Marriage means more to him, as do children. To her, home and neighbors, or study, are more important. Mercury (thinking) is in his sixth house of illness, and he gets a chance to think of it often, since she is usually sick. Her Venus is strong and she needs lots of affection. Slightly harmonious indicates fair satisfaction. His is not too strong in his chart, indicating satisfaction with a little less demonstration. His Venus is very harmonious, indicating emotional satisfaction. All in all there are enough points that it looks as though they have compatibility. Again, these thoughts are in addition to the basic comparison of magnetic, mental, and spiritual natures.

Charts 1 and 2

Charts 1 and 2 are the charts of another married couple. This marriage also has survived, though it is, perhaps on occasion, inclined to go separate ways in terms of personalities. She has a dominant Ascendant in Leo, with Moon and Uranus following it closely. The power in her chart is clustered. He has a dominant Sun in Leo, with a Leo Midheaven following and Pluto third. With her dominant Ascendant in Leo, and his Sun dominant there, there is a good basis for a basic understanding.

In regard to house placement, they share only two departments occupied: the second and the ninth. For this reason many of their activities have taken them separate ways. His Ascendant clashes with hers, but her Mars in the fifth

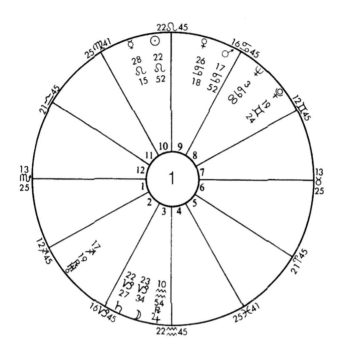

Planets — Part I			Signs -- Part II			Houses — Part III		
☉	102.75	+ 5.53	♈	19.86	- 5.63	1	61.51	- 4.63
☽	42.93	-11.70	♉	13.31	- 4.31	2	50.99	+ 2.27
☿	69.72	+ 6.08	♊	89.69	+ 8.65	3	117.50	-41.41
♀	26.62	- 8.62	♋	114.80	-26.94	4	39.66	- 4.29
♂	39.72	-11.25	♌	309.30	+20.25	5	11.31	- .39
♃	18.33	- .34	♍	34.86	+ 3.04	6	19.86	- 5.63
♄	37.49	-19.56	♎	13.31	- 4.31	7	13.31	- 4.31
♅	41.82	+ 2.44	♏	61.51	- 4.63	8	116.68	+ 7.43
♆	26.99	- 1.22	♐	50.99	+ 2.27	9	87.81	-25.72
♇	54.83	+ 5.61	♑	99.17	-41.07	10	309.30	+20.25
MC	85.45	+ 5.87	♒	57.99	- 4.63	11	34.86	+ 3.04
ASC	37.87	- 3.22	♓	11.31	- .39	12	13.31	- 4.31
Total			Total			Total		

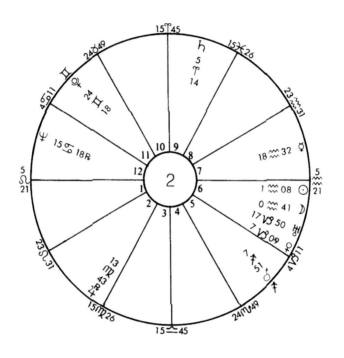

	Planets — Part I			Signs — Part II			Houses — Part III	
☉	28.97	- 4.62	♈	96.85	-10.75	1	64.82	- .28
☽	48.29	- 5.33	♉	16.53	+ .37	2	49.96	+15.22
☿	33.47	+10.27	♊	35.80	+12.25	3	16.74	+ 5.14
♀	33.05	+ .74	♋	59.67	-11.48	4	16.53	+ .37
♂	30.41	+ 7.08	♌	79.30	- 2.59	5	53.25	+15.66
♃	35.47	+17.51	♍	52.21	+22.67	6	176.51	-10.36
♄	38.00	- 2.32	♎	16.53	+ .37	7	54.77	+ 9.69
♅	47.20	+ .01	♏	14.47	+ 4.19	8	21.30	- .58
♆	35.52	- 8.81	♐	39.28	+15.85	9	55.75	- .14
♇	27.43	+ 9.68	♑	99.25	- .41	10	58.85	- 8.43
MC	43.64	-11.97	♒	153.33	- .84	11	52.33	+12.62
ASC	50.33	+ 2.03	♓	17.25	+ 2.18	12	59.67	-11.48
Total	451.78	+14.29	Total			Total		

66

house helps to satisfy the Scorpio Ascendant of his and provides an acceptable relationship when it is consummated. His power is concentrated in three houses, while hers is diffused with the exception of the sixth house. These charts show that you can make a go of dissimilar charts if the astrodynes show some basic similarities. The dominant Leo, and the fact he was out on the road often selling, helped the marriage along. If he had been home more,the dissimilar areas of environmental concentration might have caused problems which would have broken down their sense of personal and mutual pride.

Hopefully these examples will give an idea of how to use astrodynes to help determine compatibility.

As in any other area of astrology, the use of astrodynes carries with it the burden of judicious application. It must be said, though, that astrodynes can point out what is what in no uncertain terms, and can leave it to the astrologer to determine how it should be put to best use. When we have exact information, even down to the strength and harmony of the aspects, we gain precision in our deductions. You will find nothing to compare with the feeling of satisfaction gained from having pinpointed with the greatest possible accuracy the affairs of greatest and least concern—short of predicting exact events, of course.

Chapter 11

Delineating the Whole Chart

Foregoing chapters have covered such areas as temperament, compatibility, and occupation specifically as interpreted with astrodynes. In this chapter we do what well may be all too brief a delineation of a whole chart with the aid of astrodynes.

The chart used (Chart 9) has an interesting feature. The dominant planet is not what one would expect. Saturn, being angular and involved in some close aspects, is a good bet. Sun, Moon, and Mercury are angular and strongly aspected and are good other choices.

The Midheaven, as our figures show, is the strongest thing in the chart. The dominant planet is Jupiter in the second house.

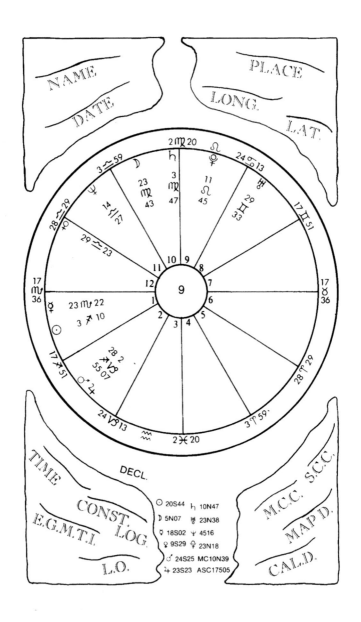

NAME

DATE

PLACE

LONG.

LAT.

2 ♍ 20   ♌   24 ♎ 13

3 ♎ 59   ☽   ♄   ♀

23 ♍ 43   3 ♍ 47   11 ♌ 45

♅

28 ♎ 29   14 ⚷ 27   29 ♊ 33   17 ♊ 51

29 ♎ 23

10   9   8

11   7

17 ♏ 36   12   9   7   17 ♉ 36

☿   1   6

23 ♏ 22   2   3   4   5

3 ♐ 10

⊙   28 ♈ 29

28 2 ♐ ♑ 55 07

17 ♐ 51   ♂ ♃

24 ♑ 13   ♒   3 ♈ 59

2 ♓ 20

DECL.

TIME

CONST.

E.G.M.T.I.   LOG.

L.O.

M.C.C. S.C.C.

MAP D.

CAL.D.

⊙	20S44	♄	10N47	
☽	5N07	♅	23N38	
☿	18S02	♆	4516	
♀	9S29	♇	23N18	
♂	24S25	MC	10N39	
♃	23S23	ASC	17S05	

70

ASTRODYNE GRAPH

	½ POWER GRILL	☉	☽	☿	♀	♂	♃	♄	♅	♆	♇	MC	ASC	
		13.97 +1.00	13.64 -1.00	14.55 +1.00	9.27 +2.00	8.31	8.30 -3.00	14.92 +1.00	10.61 +3.00	11.47	9.68 +3.00	15.00	15.00	House Power Essential Dignities
☉	25.57 -10.59			☌5.20	⊻ .22 +.28		⊻3.12 +4.68	□11.38 -17.07	⊼ .38	∠2.28 -2.28	△3.42 +3.42	□11.17 -11.17		☉
☽	22.73 -5.46	PART IV		✱7.65 +7.65		□6.80 -8.50	□3.60 -1.80		□6.17 -6.17	P 2.75	∠2.97 -2.97		✱1.88 +1.88	☽
☿	20.21 +2.81											□3.03 -3.03	☌9.23 P .75	☿
♀	16.39 +15.17					✱5.53 +5.53	✱3.27 +5.72	✱2.60 +1.95	△7.83 +9.79			✱4.05 +5.06		♀
♂	27.00 -3.41						☌6.80 MR+5.00 +6.70	△5.13 +1.26	☍9.37 P 2.33 -12.29		⚼1.83 -2.29	△6.58 +4.93	∠1.32 -1.76	♂
♃	35.92 +18.74							△8.33 +8.33	☍7.62 P 7.33 -.15		P 9.17 +4.59	△9.78 +14.67	∠4.52 -2.26	♃
♄	33.49 -7.37								✱2.77 +1.39	∠ .67 -1.00		☌10.55 P10.62 -10.59		♄
♅	30.89 -1.68										∠1.20 1.20	✱4.22 +4.22	⚼1.95 -1.95	♅
♆	11.30 -1.05										✱3.30 +3.30	∠2.12 -2.12		♆
♇	17.86 +1.85												□4.15 -4.15	♇
♂ ♇	22.43 -1.56													MC
♄ ♅	32.19 -9.05													
♃ ♆	23.61 +8.85													

PLANETS — Part I

☉	51.14	-21.14
☽	45.46	-10.91
☿	40.41	+5.62
♀	32.77	+30.33
♂	54.00	-6.42
♃	71.84	+37.48
♄	66.97	-14.73
♅	61.78	-3.36
♆	22.59	-2.10
♇	35.72	+3.70
MG	77.12	+1.97
ASC	38.80	-8.24
Total	598.60	+12.00

SIGNS — Part II

♈	54.00	-6.42
♉	16.39	+15.17
♊	81.99	-.55
♋	22.73	-5.46
♌	48.51	-1.59
♍	209.76	-20.86
♎	88.13	+58.59
♏	101.64	-4.18
♐	141.06	-8.82
♑	105.33	+30.11
♒	16.10	-4.52
♓	23.61	+8.85
Total	909.24	+60.29

HOUSES — Part III

1	152.78	-25.32
2	161.76	+49.80
3	49.58	-11.94
4	23.61	+8.85
5	27.00	-3.41
6	27.00	-3.41
7	16.39	+15.17
8	81.99	-.55
9	71.23	-7.05
10	209.76	-20.86
11	38.98	+13.07
12	49.16	+45.50
Total	909.24	+60.29

TRINITIES — Part VIII

LIFE	251.01	-35.78
WEALTH	398.52	+25.53
ASSOC	104.95	+16.30
PSYCHIC	154.76	+53.80

QUALITIES — Part VI

MOVABLE	270.19	+76.80
FIXED	182.64	+4.88
MUTABLE	456.42	-21.38

TRIPLICITIES — Part V

FIRE	243.51	-16.83
EARTH	331.40	+24.42
AIR	186.22	+53.50
WATER	147.98	-.80

SOCIETY — Part VII

PERSONAL	413.78	+58.04
COMPANIONSHIP	117.61	+17.02
PUBLIC	401.96	-15.39

CF-5

© Ken Stone, 1968

Normally an astrologer makes a quick appraisal of the overall chart before getting specific. First we observe that the Midheaven is the strongest point in the chart. We know, then, that the largest single concentration of energy in the chart will be focused on reputation and honor, business efforts, and other Midheaven affairs. We must bear in mind that the Midheaven is not an active center of energy as is a planet; it is a point at which energies find the easiest distribution to the world at large. Therefore, the manner of expression of the Midheaven, shown by the sign on the Midheaven, is still activated only by the aspects to it that make it that strong. When we delineate character, temperament, etc., we use Jupiter, which is the strongest planet. But we must remember that even stronger than Jupiter in the makeup is the focus on business efforts, reputation, honor, and other Midheaven affairs of life. In interpreting each segment of the chart, this tendency should be kept in mind; it will color the actions just as any dominant idea or passion tends to sway other affairs of life. Since we find the tenth house to be the dominant house, we will find this assessment reinforced. Note also that Virgo, ruling the Midheaven, with Saturn and the Moon therein, is also the strongest sign.

In beginning a chart delineation, we look to the trinities and quadruplicities of signs for the overall indications of temperament. A dominant Mercury in a chart with overwhelming power in earth signs is not going to show a light-headed dreamer. The overall predominance will give the types of habits and reactions most strongly evident in the person.

The strongest triplicity in the chart is earth (three planets and the Midheaven, three of which rank 1, 2, 3 in power).

Quite a ways back in second place is fire, followed more weakly with air and water close together. We can tell this person needs things to be in a practical, tangible form to handle them. She needs details; she needs to use and will use everything around her to overcome obstacles and succeed. This is especially true in endeavors where reputation is at stake, such as public affairs. The earth triplicity is harmonious, indicating that by and large these efforts and reactions are successful and well received by most people. There is enough strength in fire to give the enthusiasm to motivate others. Emotional affairs and reactions take more of a back seat. Note the discord in fire, showing less harmony in enthusing oneself and others to action. The excessive harmony in air indicates that efforts to inspire, especially in the arts, are well received.

In terms of qualities, the mutable signs are overwhelmingly predominant. This indicates considerable flexibility. To tie this fact into a practical example in the chart, consider personality—shown primarily by the first house and the planets there. Scorpio is on the Ascendant and contains Mercury in the first house. While it does contain the Sun in Sagittarius also, the Scorpio effect is predominant in the first house. It would be very easy to assume considerable fixity in the nature. Even using just the astrodynes of planets, Jupiter in a movable (cardinal) sign suggests a different approach, or conflict of testimony. Yet the mutable signs are overwhelmingly predominant. So where are we? In affairs of personality and those of a strictly personal nature, there will be the fixity shown by Scorpio, especially in speech and general communication. Appeals to the pride (Sun) can obtain some yielding. The dominant planet (the number one factor in personality) in a movable sign shows the capacity to start new efforts before others do, thereby circumventing some threats to her fixity of nature.

But regardless of personal concerns, the majority of the energy will be spent in the "to and fro" adjustments characteristic of mutable signs. This being the case, we can see possible traits begin to form: the temperament is mutable, and Ascendant and Mercury are in Scorpio. Here is a person who will go along with the desires of the moment—hers or those of others. But in so doing, she will fall back on sarcastic expression and deep moods during her activities. This is likely to be her concession to the fixity of her personality. A look at Scorpio, Sagittarius, and first house harmony shows that such activity will cause a temperament that will go along despite all her comments to the proposed activity.

Note: Nowhere in an astrological chart is anything erased, forgotten, permanently subdued (or changed to a different planetary energy). One thing astrodynes make one aware of: While certain things gain more attention than others, all parts of the chart contain energy and will express in proportion to the amount of energy available. It is our job to balance and modify, and if the power is so weak as to suggest few occurrences of its nature, it is also our job to find out how it will express in conjunction with stronger desires.

A brief look at the house groupings will give us an indication of the areas of life into which the majority of energy will be concentrated.

The triplicity of wealth predominates. This shows us that most of her energy centers in the areas of possessions and wealth, reputation or business and working environment. Even though marriage and children are in her picture, we will envision such activities as being either a job or engagement in such activities as bring honors. The trinity of life follows a poor second, showing that personal concerns and those of offspring are somewhat important. The association and psychic trinities are a distant fourth and third, showing companionship and things of a secret nature are much less important to her. The trinity of life is the only overall discordant area. As we shall see in a moment, the biggest area of difficulty is in the concerns of self.

The personal houses predominate. Note that the public houses are nearly as much. Companionship houses have very little energy. First and foremost are personal concerns, followed closely by public affairs. Considering that the first house is the most discordant, as are the trinity of life, personal concerns cause most discord. Let us keep in mind that the activity of the house (the houses being reactive factors rather than active factors) indicates only the strength of energy which attracts a person to the area of life where the events of the indicated nature can be made to happen!

We may also assess the person's most frequent methods of expression by noting the predominant signs. Virgo is the dominant sign in the chart, indicating critical faculty and fondness for details. As the most discordant sign in the chart it shows a tendency to hypercriticism. The second strongest sign is Sagittarius, giving a tendency to bluntness and freely given opinion. It also gives a tendency to look at things in terms of nature and faith.

The Chart in Detail

At the risk of sounding like a soapbox orator, let us state one more time why dominant planets, signs, and houses play a large part in delineation even when conventional rules might ignore them (as in a dominant planet affecting personality even if not in the first house or aspecting the rulers of the first house)

The strongest energy in the chart will push for the greatest amount of expression and recognition. Strongest desires find most frequent expression; any psychologist will likely agree. The same principle is true in every arena of human endeavor. In this chart it is folly to predict ongoing despondency (although periods of it are indicated) with a dominant Jupiter, for the Jupiterian characteristics will surface faster than any other with this person. In the same manner of speaking, both Neptune and Uranus are in succeedent houses. To expect, in view of the astrodynes, that idealism will play an equal part to individualistic behavior, or that friendship will show more prominence in the affairs involving other people's money, is unrealistic. Moreover, the life will not bear out such ideas.

Temperament

The factors to consider here are, again:

- The dominant planet.
- Personality, as shown by the Ascendant and planets in the first house.
- Mentality, as shown by the Moon and aspects.
- Character, as shown by the Sun and aspects.

Jupiter in Capricorn is the dominant force in the temperament. This person will always retain an optimistic approach to life. She will operate on the assumption that someone or something will always help out in a pinch. This person will be good at getting others to join an endeavor, and will be especially adept at getting those in a position of authority or of benefit to her to cooperate in her efforts. This person will always retain faith in the Creator, even though it will relate to the more practical affairs of life. This person can be generous. Above all, this person is well organized. Since we observe aspects leading to worry and difficulty, it is important to note that, while she may sound worried or upset, she will still maintain the faith that things will work out, that someone or something will save the day. Jupiter is in the second house, showing that possessions and monetary affairs have a strong bearing on the jovial and beneficent mood, that it is through this area that the temperament is most easily stimulated. In other words, events and conditions surrounding possessions and acquisition; expenditure of wealth or possessions are the strongest conditions affecting the expression of the temperament.

We have no room to analyze each aspect. Note that the house position of Jupiter is a house that is the next to the weakest in a chart; it is the aspects that have made Jupiter so active. Looking to see which aspects are strongest and most affecting the temperament, we see a trine from Saturn, a parallel from Pluto, a trine to the Midheaven, and finally an opposition and parallel from Uranus. The strongest traits then are organizational ability; ability to get cooperation from others; ability to gain recognition through the jovial approach to selling others on self and ideas. There is an ability to advertise self or others' affairs to advantage. There is a great deal of desire for independence and original work—especially in those endeavors relating to fund-raising and other efforts in behalf of charities and organizations. While there is some sacrifice involved which disturbs personal comfort, the results are generally good (note the total discord of Jupiter opposition Uranus and Jupiter parallel Uranus is only -.15). These are not the only aspects worthy of consideration; they are the aspects our graph shows to be the strongest. These traits will be most notable. Observe that a semisextile to the Sun by Jupiter is nearly as strong as the Moon-Jupiter square.

The next step in judging temperament is to judge the personality. Scorpio rules the Ascendant. Mercury in Scorpio and Sun in Sagittarius are in the first house. The general rule is that planets in the house are considered first unless the ruler of the house by sign is at least twice as strong. A look at the astrodynes shows that the Sun is the strongest, then Mercury, and then the Ascendant. Since the rulers of the house by sign total less than Sun, Mercury, or Ascendant, the rule holds. We know now that in this chart the chief ruler of the first house is not the one closest to the cusp of the first house. Since the Sun shows the character (deep-seated traits) of this person (step 4), we can see that the character traits are an integral part of the personality and quite strong. Pride and self-esteem are important. This makes for a strong-willed person. She will be frank and outspoken.

We might think she was adamant, even; but we remember the overwhelming amount of mutable quality and decide instead that she will tend to change from one position to another according to what will bring her the greatest amount of attention. Again there is the indication of generosity—though somewhat at war with secret elements in the nature. Since we find Mercury and Ascendant in Scorpio, we can see the forthright and frank nature combining with Scorpio sarcasm to give very blunt and biting comments of a personal nature. The graph shows us that her expression of sarcasm and bluntness are detrimental to her, more than any area in the chart.

The most outstanding aspects to the Sun are the squares to Saturn and the Midheaven. These show a tendency to worry, along with a bit of inferiority complex which is compensated by tearing apart other people. Virgo on the Midheaven heightens the tendency to hypercriticism, which reaches blunt and sometimes brutal proportions in the openness of Sagittarius.

Mercury is very interesting. There are but five aspects, one being a weak parallel. Yet the aspects involved not only give the widest expression available, they are strong enough to give Mercury a fair amount of power. A conjunction to the Sun gives outward expression to innermost feelings. A sextile to the Moon gives good recall and an immediate tap to all capacities in the subconscious. A conjunction to the Ascendant gives maximum facility to outward physical efforts of communication. The square to the Midheaven indicates some difficulties, but rounds out the ability to objective expression to the widest number of people. Do not expect a wider variety of abilities to show up in the objective mental processes; with the Moon slightly stronger and with more aspects, look for hunches and subconscious processes to pop up with answers.

The mental capacities (Moon) and ability to understand are colored by Virgo, giving a strong tendency to analyze and criticize many areas. Though the power leader of the lower half of the planets, the Moon has seven aspects. The capacity for mathematics, courage to fight for what one believes, a feeling for music and dramatics, and a sense of time are shown. Strongest aspects are a square to Mars and Uranus completing a T-square. This shows a quick temper and a desire to break the domestic mold. The temper affects the mental capacities most strongly when finances are involved. Sudden changes in other people's money causes nervousness and consequently sudden changes. In other words, other people (Uranus) cause many changes which may be stumbling blocks. These blocks force a change of thinking and broaden the horizons, even if causing nervous frustration.

The other strong aspect is Mercury sextile the Moon. This gives good recall and the ability to express what is understood. It gives a tendency to play hunches, which are usually fairly accurate. A harmonious Moon-Mercury aspect can help a great deal with expressive capabilities if Mercury does not have a great many aspects, and the Moon has a variety. The harmonious aspect indicates a good link between the subconscious and the conscious. In this manner those qualities and characteristics that form the mental capacities for understanding that do not have direct access to the calculative facilities shown by Mercury aspects are provided the opportunity for reaching the objective mind.

Possessions

The second house is the second strongest in the chart and contains the dominant planet. Acquisition of wealth, whether monetary or possessions, plays an important part in the whole outlook on life. Usually we would say, by rule of thumb, that the first planet in the house is the chief ruler. But astrodynes show us that the second planet, Jupiter, is substantially stronger than the first planet, Mars. We would take Jupiter as the chief ruler of affairs of wealth. This shows optimism and the ability to obtain patronage. It gives the ability to sell at advantage. Jupiter generally attracts money. Since Jupiter is the most harmonious planet in the chart, there is a high degree of attractive ability in regard to wealth. At worst, there is sufficient, even in times of difficulty, to see her through to better times.

Since Mars is here and fairly strong and conjunct Jupiter, there is a strong tendency to extravagance. Mars and Jupiter in the second house combined with the second most harmonious planet in the twelfth house (Venus) sextile Mars and Jupiter indicate working with hospitals and institutions as lucrative. Superiors can reward well also.

As shown by astrodynes, the most destructive trait in regard to wealth is impatience and a tendency to blow up at the least little thing (Mars opposition, parallel Uranus). The explosive, combative attitude is good to stir activity. Since Venus in the twelfth house conciliates the Mars opposition Uranus (Venus trine Uranus, sextile Mars), it shows again that service to others can harmoniously unite the opposition while using the drive and steam of the opposition.

The second house is the most harmonious, showing that the greatest share of pleasure comes through mental and physical possessions. A Sun slightly less strong than Mars and discordant shows that being in business for oneself (the ability to attract gold) is not a desirable factor in the chart. Likewise the Moon, with its attractive ability toward silver and working with the general public, is shown to be less desirable in attracting wealth (Moon afflicted-discordant).

Studies, Neighbors, and Relatives

A misconception that is prevalent among some astrologers is that people will be shown by such and such a house measured from such and such a house. By this rule, everyone's father and grandmother will be the fourth house, everyone's mother and grandfather will be the tenth house, and the partner's relatives will be just the opposite; nephews and nieces the eighth house; grandchildren the ninth house, etc. Every house gets into the act. In truth the rationale becomes hard to justify. Certain close relatives—legal or blood—are shown by other houses because of the marked effect on the person: wife or husband, children, mother and father. The rest of the relatives of any variety are shown by the third house. Not only brothers and sisters are shown, but all other relatives.

In this chart the third house is one of the weakest in the chart and is the third most discordant house in the chart. This indicates there is not a great deal of energy spent in these directions—and that which does end up with more discord than most other areas in life. Most of the power making the house rate above the fourth, fifth, and sixth is due to Aquarius being intercepted. Saturn, as ruler of Capricorn on the cusp and co-ruler of Aquarius, also stronger than Uranus, must be considered the main ruler of the house. The strongest aspect is Sun square Saturn. This shows a basic indisposition toward both neighbors and relatives, primarily due to a conflict between her ego and her concern for her mother's opinions (Saturn in the tenth house). Uranus, receiving oppositions from Mars and Jupiter as strongest aspects, shows considerable impatience with relationships of a reasonably close nature. With the second and eighth houses involved, we can assume that money matters may have considerable effect on this feeling. This same impatience will carry over in the short distance traveling necessary to everyday affairs.

Home Life

In general, the fourth house shows indications of home life, the effect it has upon the subconscious, the intimate conditions found surrounding one from birth to death. Interestingly, the fourth house rules the father - probably because the mental concept of the father is vague and buried in the psyche much like the fourth house is the most hidden in the chart, and much unlike the tenth house, ruling the mother, the most exposed house in the chart.

In this birth chart, the fourth house is the second weakest house. Pisces is the ruler of the cusp. Home and home conditions do not demand a great deal of attention from this person. Since this person is married and takes care of a home very well, we must make a point here. Adherence to the duty imposed upon one by the environment is one thing (and reinforced by her Scorpio rising sense of duty); being wrapped up in the home and doing things to or for it is another. It is the latter point of view that is weak. Since Jupiter is more than three times as strong as Neptune, the Jupiter influence will predominate and lend some harmony as well. The trine of Saturn and the Midheaven are the strongest aspects, showing the relationship with the mother as the greatest effect—with reputation and other superiors as second in line. It also shows that pride of possession plus a bit of austerity (Saturn) create a harmonious atmosphere. Jupiter parallel Pluto indicates an effect on home from publicity, longer travels, and philosophy of life—an effect which is upbeat.

Love Affairs, Children, and Entertainment

Again, this is a weak house involved with affairs of the heart and social gatherings. Since Aries rules the sixth house also, we might as well look at the indications as applied to sickness, employees, small animals, etc. Mars ruling Aries shows the energetic, passionate approach to both areas of life. Conjunct Jupiter, it gives good vitality and the ability to recuperate quickly from an illness and expenditure of energy. Opposition to Uranus shows an unorthodox approach to love, which can sometimes backfire; in sixth house affairs, nervous exhaustion can come about from exasperation with others who do not put forth the amount of effort she does and expects from others.

(When delineating aspects to a ruler of a house, it is easy to give full weight to each aspect, which gives an importance that is out of proportion to actuality. By observing astrodynes, one can get the relative importance of each area. Each characteristic shown by the aspects to the house ruler will have an effect commensurate with portions of the total power o the planet it represents. However, the total importance of each of those traits in relation to the whole chart is shown by the power of the house.)

Again we note that a weak house does not preclude affairs of the house. There are two children. What it does show is that affairs relating to children or entertainment or love affairs, etc., do not demand a greater portion of energy expression in this area.

Marriage, Partners, Open Enemies

The seventh house is the best in the chart. Being ruled by Taurus on the cusp, it is harmonious (third most harmonious). Again we see little of planetary energy seeking this area as an outlet. Further, we note this weak a house did not show lack of marriage. There is a husband. Strongest aspect to Venus, ruler of the seventh house, is a trine from Uranus. This shows ingenuity and magnetism to attract the partner. It also shows that the partner's money can harmoniously contribute to the marriage well being. Next strongest is a sextile from Mars, showing passion and affection mixing harmoniously.

Death, Inheritance, Psychic Affairs,
and Others' Money

The eighth house is the significator here. It is the fourth strongest house. The ruler of the house, Uranus, is the fourth strongest planet. It shows sudden changes. Intuition is indicated and is especially useful in fund-raising as well as everyday affairs. The heaviest aspects are oppositions and parallels from Mars and Jupiter. Bad personal money judgment may cause some of the problem, causing a drain on the partner's money. A trine from Venus in the twelfth house, conciliating the opposition, shows help from sudden and unexpected sources can save the day. If nothing else, events will occur through the actions of other people.

Teaching, Publicity, Long
Travels, and Philosophy

The ninth house is occupied by Pluto and is the fifth strongest house in the chart, even though Pluto is weak. The strongest aspect is a parallel from Jupiter. In itself, Jupiter in Capricorn would give a conservative streak to the religious philosophy which would otherwise be more inclined to metaphysical ideas. Jupiter in the second house shows a more materialistic trend. Yet this house also rules teaching. She teaches music, combining the ninth house expression with the second. She also has been employed as a church organist.

Therefore, the materialistic or monetary trend gets its outlet in an acceptable manner. The next strongest aspect is a square to the Ascendant, showing a tendency to want to force personal ideas on others. Since Pluto is harmonious (+3.70), the overall efforts to gain cooperation are successful, especially if the tongue can be held from sarcasm (Scorpio on the Ascendant). Because the ninth house is discordant, it is likely that long trips do not meet with a lot of success or pleasure overall, though some spots may seem bright.

Business Affairs, Honor,
Reputation, and Mother

All of the above affairs belong primarily to the tenth house. The tenth house is the strongest in the chart, as is the sign of Virgo, which is on the tenth house cusp. The Midheaven is the strongest point in the chart. This combination points out that this person will naturally draw herself to the environment of business and honor more frequently than any other. This factor also shows that the mother has a very strong effect on the person's actions, whether overtly or covertly.

(Someone else's opinion of a person and the person's own opinion frequently differ. The birthchart does not necessarily show something as others see it, as much as it does an individual's own feeling and reactions to an event or situation.

Because the Midheaven represents the point where the energies and efforts of the individual are most easily given off to the world at large—publicized, if you will—it is apparent that doing something of note or working in an occupation or avocation is very important. That is, there will be strong associations with "how popular or well known will this make me?" with a wide variety of events.)

Overall, the strongest aspect here is Saturn conjunct (10.55) and parallel (10.62) the Midheaven. Outside of working with and for older people, it shows a conservative trend and a tendency to want to be the center of things—to have everything come to self. Whether efforts of a business nature or efforts in the community, it shows a well organized, highly detailed approach to reach the top. Insofar as the mother is concerned, it shows a mother whom she considered as highly critical. Conversely, she tends to reply in a similar manner.

The strongest aspect to the Midheaven is the square from the Sun. Likewise, the strongest aspect to Saturn is also the square form the Sun. This shows a tendency to have problems with superiors: Saturn square Sun shows a basic inner tendency to an inferiority complex (or at least worry about self-worth); Sun square Midheaven shows a tendency to overcompensate with pride. Both attitudes cause difficulty, especially as the afflictions are to Saturn and the Midheaven in Virgo, where hypercritical nature combines with the bluntness of the Sagittarius Sun. The Moon in the tenth house (Virgo) shows the subconscious reactions with a similar tendency.

A strong sextile from Mercury here shows that resourceful thinking (Scorpio) will be of great help in mitigating the difficulty—and also with working with the general public, although not strong enough to overcome the discord. Our graph shows harmonious support from Venus, Mars, Jupiter, and Uranus to Saturn and the Midheaven and shows help from money areas (second house: Mars, Jupiter; eighth house: Uranus) and unseen sources (Venus in the twelfth house).

Note in the Midheaven column that we have two sextiles stronger than the squares.

Friends, Acquaintances, and Ambitions

The eleventh house, being occupied by Neptune, is stronger than the empty houses. Still it is the fourth house from the weakest house. While there are strongly idealistic feelings about friends (Neptune), there is not much energy working toward events in this area. Neptune is the weakest planet in the chart. It is also discordant. It shows a confused attitude toward friends and an uncertain nature regarding hopes. More is hoped than realized. When relations are good, there is stronger pleasure experienced. This is normal delineation. The important thing to notice with astrodynes is that there is very little energy working toward these things regardless of the fact the house is occupied. In contrast, note that the third house is unoccupied and is stronger than the eleventh house. Therefore, third house affairs will be more prominent than eleventh house affairs, despite the fact the eleventh house is occupied by a planet.

Self-created Disappointments, Hidden Enemies, Institutions, and Psychic Affairs

The twelfth house is occupied by Venus. The house is not powerful; the third house, mentioned above, is a tiny bit stronger. It does contain the second most harmonious planet (and also second weakest). While there will not be a great deal of activity, in the area of hidden enemies and relations with institutions and elemental psychic affairs, what occurs is good for this person. While there is sufficient discord to provide disappointment, those types of difficulties created by the desire to remain out of sight (twelfth house) of self-imagined limitations (twelfth house) are not a source of difficulty. On the contrary, there is the ability to sense whether a situation is right for certain actions or not. A trine from Uranus in the eighth house is the strongest aspect and shows a developed intuition and charm in working with people. Also, she can rally support form the elemental side of life.

Other Considerations

In rushing through delineation this quickly we did not cover all pertinent factors to events shown by some houses. For instance, in questions of wealth, the Sun and Moon strength and harmony should be considered. They delineate the ability to attract the metals which underlie our currency, as well as whether wealth can be attracted by self-employment or better by the employment of others. Jupiter and Saturn can have an influence if selling or buying is involved. In this case (wealth), these factors should be compared in strength and in harmony to the factors of the pertinent houses to get a complete answer.

In health, both the first and sixth houses are involved and should be weighed in order to get the proper assessment. Even then, planets that are weak and discordant are potential areas of health difficulties. Therefore, our astrodyne graph will give you an index of the areas of greatest health concern. Sun, Saturn, Moon, and Ascendant are most discordant in our chart. In general, heart or back ailments would rank high, with chronic ailment and cancer of intestines stronger. There will also be a tendency to female disorders.

Likewise, any strongly harmonious aspect is a source of wealth, if its abilities and characteristics are tapped.

With a discordant planet or a discordant house (or combination) there may be at least one relatively harmonious, strong aspect which the person can consciously work to associate with afflicted areas of life which will bring the greatest amount of good possible under the circumstances.

As an example, Neptune has only one harmonious aspect, a sextile to Pluto. Relationships on a friendly or associate basis, when associated with teaching or public expression, can create the most harmonious situation available when Neptune is involved in eleventh house affairs.

These are just a few of the way astrodynes can be used in delineation. As every practicing astrologer knows, a thorough delineation in so few pages is difficult to do. It would be equally difficult to go into every possible nuance to be gleaned from the astrodyne graph.

If we remember, as so often stated, that the prominence of any event or trait indicated in the chart is in direct proportion to the amount of energy straining for expression, we will put all the factors in their rightful places. And if we remember that large doses of harmony or discord will become prominent only to the extent there is enough power to produce the harmonious or discordant results, our delineation will arrive at the closest approximations available of the person it describes.

Mathematical efforts such as astrodynes do not always appeal to the more romantic-minded astrologers, but those who have utilized the astrodynes in delineation generally feel a keener grasp on the makeup of the person involved. Some also feel a security in having facts to back suppositions. Whatever the case, we hope this book has helped readers apply the astrodyne method in their delineations.